SWANS

SWANS

words by

JACK DENTON SCOTT

photographs by

OZZIE SWEET

G. P. PUTNAM'S SONS NEW YORK

Some action photographs
of adult swans in flight were taken by Diane Sweet.

Text copyright © 1987 by Jack Denton Scott
Illustrations copyright © 1987 by Ozzie Sweet
All rights reserved. Published simultaneously in
Canada by General Publishing Co. Limited, Toronto.
Printed in the United States of America
Book design by Kathleen Westray

Library of Congress Cataloging-in-Publication Data

Scott, Jack Denton.
Swans/words by Jack Denton Scott; photographs by Ozzie Sweet.
p.   cm.
Summary: Text and photographs depict the physical characteristics,
behavior, and life cycle of swans in their natural habitat.
ISBN 0-399-21406-2
1. Swans—Juvenile literature.   [1. Swans.]
I. Sweet, Ozzie, ill. II. Title.
QL696.A52S35   1987
598.4'1—dc19   87-20447   CIP   AC

First Impression

This, my eighteenth wildlife book,
is dedicated with admiration and affection
to my daughters, PAMELA and LINNEA,
and to my son, BLAIR.
Thank you for your interest and support
through the years, and for spending
so much time helping in the field
while I produced the photography
for many of the books.

—OS

A S A SYMBOL of beauty, grace and power, the swan has always excited the artistic imagination. It was a favorite subject of Michelangelo and Leonardo da Vinci in their handsome paintings of the Greek myth of Leda and the Swan, and of the twentieth-century Irish poet Yeats in his controversial poem "Leda and the Swan." And it is the gracefulness of the swan that inspired one of the most popular of all classical ballets, *Swan Lake,* and Tchaikovsky's stirring swan music.

But while the swan is the embodiment of grace in paintings, poetry, music and dance, it is at the pond or lake or along the coastline that you see the swan at its best—in its natural beauty.

There are seven species of this, our most dramatic bird, coming from such widely varied areas as Asia, Australia, South America, Europe and North America.

Five are large, majestic and white. The largest is the trumpeter, weighing up to 40 pounds and having an overall length of about five feet and a wingspread that can reach as much as eight feet. Bewick, mute, whistling and whooper swans are also big birds, each weighing over 25 pounds, and with wingspreads not much smaller than the trumpeter's.

The remaining two species, the South American black-necked and Australian black swans, differ dramatically from the pure white bird most of us are used to seeing.

Trumpeter

Bewick

Mute

Whistling swan

South American black-necked swan

Whooper

Australian black swan

Swans are not just decorative birdlife that grace lakes, ponds and coast-lines; they are also accomplished flyers. In fact, their sometimes magnificently long or high flight is considered by ornithologists to be the most astonishing flight of all birds. This may not be surprising when you consider that a swan's wingspan is longer than the length of its body from the tip of its bill to the end of its tail! Aided by powerful chest muscles, the swan's wings beat with a precise, almost machinelike regularity of motion at 160 flaps a minute (compared to ducks that must flap over 300 times a minute). Their flight speeds vary from 18 miles an hour on local flights to over 55 miles an hour on migratory travels, and they soar at ranges from 50 to 500 feet locally, and from 2,000 to 10,000 feet or higher on longer travels. These are the averages, but there are startling exceptions: The migratory Bewick swan regularly flies 2,600 miles from breeding grounds in Siberia to England and elsewhere in Europe, and a whistling swan was struck by an airplane at 30,000 feet!

On long flights, swans, like geese, fly in V formations, each swan behind the leader receiving some free lift from the slipstream created by the lead bird and the bird directly in front. Experts explain that in this migratory flight pattern, a certain portion of air spills over the wing tips of each bird, resulting in a loss of valuable air lift. Simultaneously, however, this spilled air spins into a growing spiral, a vortex directly behind each wing tip, resulting in an air surge on the outer edges of the wings. In this migrational flying formation, each bird flies behind but slightly to one side of the bird ahead, momentarily resting its inner wing tip on the rising current from the bird in front. This supplies some lift for the bird following and utilizes some of that wing energy lost by the bird in front. What this flight formation accomplishes is the conservation of energy of all but the lead bird. But as swans change leaders periodically, the arrowlike V-flight benefits the whole flock.

When there are strong, flight-impeding head winds over water, the swans decrease altitude, taking advantage of the fact that nearer the water the wind is slowed down by the friction created by the waves, thus making flying easier.

The wings that create the swan's remarkable flight are composed of the humerus bone (the upper arm), attached at the elbow to the radius and ulna bones (the forearm). Similar to our own arm, the swan's wing has a wrist that joins a hand. The swan's hand has just three fingers and is covered with feathers so it is difficult to see. The first finger and thumb connect where the hand joins the wrist, and the long second finger is the wing tip. The swan's flight is also made possible by the wing bones, which are hollow. These "floating" bones are covered with a thin, strong skin on which the flight feathers grow.

Eleven almost metal-stiff primary feathers on the wing tips are a vital part of the swan's propulsion. These major feathers are narrower at the ends of the quill than they are on the wider so-called "vanes" on the rear. Consequently, when the wings downstroke, the feathers fan open like fingers, and more air pressure—thus power—is forced on the wider vanes, causing each primary feather to twist like a propeller. These broader-vane feathers are complicated structures of hundreds of barbs or filaments.

The entire body of the swan is masked with small contour feathers, which create its unique shape and also provide superb insulation. All of these feathers are activated by skin muscles connected to feather follicles that raise and lower feathers, and even move them sideways, to assist in flight.

Thus, the miracle of flight is made possible by a complicated collection of more than 25,000 feathers with many individual functions, all powered by muscles. In comparison, an aircraft is a clumsy, simple machine that bumbles noisily across the skies.

Those tightly fitted feathers, however, are not only responsible for efficient flight; they also help keep the swan afloat, and warm and dry. Meticulous regarding their appearance, swans bathe daily, splashing water over themselves, then drying their feathers by flapping their wings and shaking their bodies vigorously. Then they preen. Sometimes before preening they even take off in flight to dry completely. They look like they are walking on water before takeoff.

One researcher reported that in a 13-hour period an adult swan preened five times and bathed once. A complete, careful preening took from 21 to 40 minutes, with some swans faster than others, and others not quite so particular.

Swans employ their bill and head feathers to collect oil from the preen gland at the base of the tail. It protrudes like a wick and is surrounded by a downy tuft. Both bill and head feathers distribute the preening oil to all of the plumage. The oil contains fatty acid, fat and wax, which help prevent feathers from drying and fraying, while at the same time conditioning the surface of the bill.

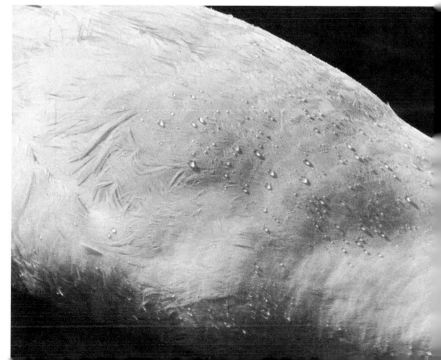

At least that was the theory for years. Today, however, scientists have changed their minds about the waterproofing provided by preening. Contending that nonaquatic birds also have similar oil glands, they now believe that the oil gland is a major source of Vitamin D that is ingested during preening. Experiments have concluded that evenly distributed air captured in the barbules of the feathers is mainly responsible for the waterproofing.

Those well-cared-for wings have yet another function: In conjunction with the bill, they are effective defense weapons. A large, bony knuckle at the exact bend of the wing becomes a powerful bludgeon when needed. All swans are aggressive and motivated strongly by territorial imperatives, fiercely driving off and sometimes even killing intruders that enter the 12-acre territory that they consider theirs and defend.

They have been known (mutes especially, which are the most aggressive) to drown even large dogs, subduing them with wing blows, then using their large wings to push and hold the dogs underwater. So fierce and strong are their wing blows that one male mute actually crushed a heavy galvanized bucket that was being used as a shield against the bird's attack.

Swans guarding nests have many times attacked and broken the legs of men who approached their young or tried to steal their eggs from the nest.

So swans, whose beauty changes a pond or lake into a ballet, are competently armed and equipped for survival. But for the most part these remarkable birds use their physical assets in positive ways.

The bill, which aids in preening and defense, is also a necessary tool for feeding. Consisting of a tight, overlapping layer of soft skin, just the tip, the "nail," is horny and thick. The serrated edges of the mandibles that form the bill make it easy for swans to tear off stalks and leaves of marine plants upon which they subsist. Adults eat from eight to fourteen pounds of vegetation daily.

Large webbed feet on short legs, positioned near the rear of their bodies, become powerful paddles propelling them through the water easily and speedily. Located too far from the bird's center of gravity, however, those legs make walking on land difficult.

Their feet have other important functions. Three strong, nailed toes are advantageous for digging in the shallow bottoms of ponds and lakes to uproot vegetation. Standing in the water, they rake those nailed feet back and forth, and then return to a floating position on the water's surface to pull up the loose or uprooted plants.

The webbed feet may not function so well on land, but on water they do everything except actually walk on the surface. On takeoff on their water runway, swans require about five seconds to get into the air, their large webbed feet pushing backward hard against the water, their wings beating strongly. When aloft, and at cruising speed, they pull feet and legs up and back under their bodies, streamlining the body and smoothing the flight. In this position, the toes stretch back almost to the tip of the tail.

Landing on water, they push their webbed feet forward as brakes, assisting the rapid motion of their stop-motion, back-beating wings. With the largest of our waterfowl, both takeoff and landing are impressive sights of maximum effort of timing and motion.

Takeoff on land

Admirably equipped for their diet of water plants, their high, wide skull and extremely powerful jaw muscles enable swans to yank plants up from even deeper water. The combination of the bill's hard nail and rough tongue, also with serrated edges, makes it possible not only to grip their food firmly, but also to break it up easily.

Besides its overall graceful aspect, the swan has an amazing number of vertebrae—60 in all, with 25 in the neck alone. No other bird or mammal—including the giraffe—has more vertebrae.

Tipping their bottoms high above the water, their heads underwater, these unique birds use that powerfully flexible neck to drive their bills deep into the water for those aquatic plants that are their main fare, although they sometimes get variety by eating marine insect larvae, snails and even small fish.

Unlike ducks, however, swans do not dive very often, even when seeking food. Although they are as skillful at diving as ducks are, they reserve that action, using it only when danger threatens.

They lack the true crop of most birds, having instead a long, narrow gullet and special glands in the stomach to store food that is later ground into a pulp by a large, oval-shaped gizzard, which is actually a grinding stomach.

Their highly developed senses of hearing and sight are an early-warning system that makes swans keenly aware of danger in any form. Hearing is very acute: One observer reported that a pair of swans heard a soft footfall over 200 yards away.

The eyesight of swans is keen because they have a retina twice as thick as man's, which adjusts easily to changes in light intensity and on which images are focused quickly and effectively. Swans have a third eyelid, the protective nictitating membrane, which covers the eyes when the lids are open and acts somewhat like a windshield wiper, clearing rain and fog from their vision, and shielding their eyes underwater. Their wide field of both monocular and binocular vision is greater to the sides than straight ahead. But overall, swans have a most effective full visual field; they are able to detect motion, sight and danger from all sides.

The swan also has a voice, and perhaps the most controversial of swan stories or legends centers around the swan's voice. This is the belief in the "swan song," in the swan's breaking into a beautiful, soft song just before it dies. We have perpetuated this belief by incorporating the term "swan song" into our modern language, using it to describe a final action, often of a politician whose last act in office is called his swan song.

The belief that a swan sings a sad song just before it dies goes back to 370 B.C. and the Dialogues of Plato in which Socrates discussed the Song of the Dying Swan. In fact, before he himself died, Socrates said, "You do not think that I can see as far ahead as a swan. You know that when swans feel the approach of death, they sing—and they sing sweeter and louder on the last days of their lives because they are going back to that god whom they serve."

At one time, in exploring the swan-song belief, 4,000 whistling swans were legally killed in the United States, and there were no dying songs from any of them. It is a fact, however, that the lungs of both the whooper and whistling swans collapse when they die, with their windpipes sending forth a last faint, flutelike, strange melancholy sound.

Dr. Daniel Elliott, a renowned ornithologist, and one of the founders of New York's American Museum of Natural History, shot a whistling swan for the museum. As the bird came tumbling down in its last flight, Dr. Elliott was astounded to hear a plaintive, musical song, completely unlike any sound the bird made in life, the strange song lasting until the bird reached the water.

Dr. John T. Zimmer, also of the Museum of Natural History, has a few possible explanations. He believes that a last burst of air, passing through the long convoluted windpipe of a swan that is dying, could produce a soft, seemingly sad musical note. He also reports that it is possible that the swan's trachea was pierced by shotgun pellets, preventing a normal amount of air from reaching the voice box and thus producing an odd final sound. But the mystery continues: Dr. Albert Hochbaum, a noted waterfowl scientist, writing in his authoritative book *The Travels and Traditions of Waterfowl*, concurs in the ancient and modern belief of the dying swan's song. The dying swan, he says, does indeed sing a sad last song.

Our most popular swan—the one most of us know, the mute—makes its song, a cellolike sound, with its wings. While the very name of the bird indicates that it makes no voice sounds at all, at the English swannery Abbotsbury, west of the Isle of Wight, it was discovered that the mute was far from voiceless, emitting eight distinct sounds. This includes a deep trumpeting, a shrill alarm call, a defense cry, a victory call from males after besting rivals and a distinct yelping from females to summon their young. Mute? Someone made a mistake. These are just swans that know when to keep their mouths shut. They make noises and communicate only when necessary.

Although all seven species of swans have their own individual characteristics and are impressive members of the clan, the mute is the one most of us see, and is the most historically familiar, dating back to before the Middle Ages. The mute is also the most durable, having been known to live to age seventy, nearly twice as long as the other species.

In addition, most ornithologists rate the mute as the most beautiful of all swans, not only because of its gleaming white plumage and lordly bearing on the water—which it seems to control much as a seaman masters his ship—but because of the graceful S-curve of its neck. This arching neck quickly identifies the mute, as it is the only swan to have it.

Mutes can be instantly identified, both male and female, by a large black knob at the base of an orange bill. They are also the only swans that carry their long, pointed tails in a slightly uptilted position; all others have a downward-curved tail. The mute is a surprisingly long bird, measuring 50 to 60 inches from the tip of its bill to the end of its tail. At 18 to 35 pounds (some few even weighing over 40 pounds), the male mute is, along with the trumpeter, the heaviest of all flying birds.

The mute can fly up to 50 miles an hour but doesn't like to fly as high as the other swans and, with much webbed foot–pushing and wing-flapping, needs about 30 feet of runway space to take off from the water.

Although the mute was imported to this country from Europe as a domesticated bird to ornament estates, lakes and ponds, it is known today throughout much of the United States as a wild migrating bird. Being birds of good sense, mute swans will, if fed on lakes and ponds, generally stay put and enjoy the handout. Some of the mutes escape from their beauty-aid roles (provided they are not pinioned so they cannot fly), and their young that can fly reproduce in the wild, where they ably survive without the aid of man.

By migrating, mutes are doing what comes naturally; for centuries the mute has bred in the wild all over the world: the British Isles, Denmark, Scandinavia, Germany, Poland, Russia, and ranges throughout Asia Minor, Iran, Turkestan, Mongolia and Siberia. In the winter, the mute leaves its cold breeding ranges and flies to southern Europe, Africa, southwestern Asia, even Korea and India.

Thus, the mute is an internationally known swan, respected everywhere for its stately grace, survival ability and family allegiance. When most of us describe a swan, it is the mute—the common denominator of all swans, although there is nothing common about the bird. In fact, in England not only are mutes the royalty of birdlife, but at one time only royalty could own them.

The mute has had the protection of the Crown and has been a Royal Bird in Britain for over 800 years. When that declaration was sealed by royal decree, the king had the privilege of presenting swans as gifts, and all swans were legally owned. The law stated that swans could be kept only on private waters, that they were to be pinioned and marked, and that they were the property of the owners of those waters who were permitted to recapture them if they escaped.

As swans were Royal Birds, owners enjoyed unusual prestige; possession of them was a status symbol. The swan markings of ownership were similar to cattle brands in the United States. Initially, there were about 1,000 marks in use, and they were inscribed on the upper mandible of the beak. Scars were actually formed by cutting through the skin of the swan's beak with a sharp knife, then pulling off the skin between the incisions. More complicated designs were burned in with a small branding iron. The marks were most commonly arrows, crossbows, swords or marks suggestive of the owner's name or heraldic device, or special symbols the owner favored. All swan marks were protected by law and were registered in swan-rolls (dating back to 1492) of each area. While some swan marks are still in use and valid today, the Royal Swans of the Court are no longer marked. They are, however, still managed by a Swan Master, who was, and still is, in charge of "swan-upping," an annual swan roundup just before the flight stage of young swans. While gone are the days when swan-upping was centered around a great flotilla of over 2,000 swans floating down the Thames River pursued by some of England's finest, today's ceremony of catching and identifying the birds is nevertheless a colorful and regal two-week event.

In the United States we were more practical in our association with the swan—mainly the wild trumpeter and whistling swans. In the late eighteenth century the Hudson's Bay Company began an active trade in swan skins, a lucrative business that extended into the next century and to the western states. Swans' down became famous for powder puffs, and the quills were considered the best for writing pens. In an ironic twist, even John James Audubon, that famous painter of beautiful birds, admitted that birds weren't in the same class with swans and declared he would use nothing but a swan-quill pen for his fine detail work.

Today, however, swans on the water, wild and free, or yachting along as only they can on privately owned ponds or lakes, or on waters in parks, are even more appreciated than fine paintings. A pair of swans with their family of young swimming serenely along, male and female handsomely in charge, is one of nature's most stirring sights.

Swans mature at three to four years and begin pair formation in the fall. A family begins when a male swan, called a "cob," and a female, the "pen," size one another up and make at first tentative and then final selections. Later, prior to breeding, the birds gently rub heads and necks and engage in a repetitious dipping of head and neck into the water. They then begin a stylized and synchronized head dipping. When that is accomplished, often the male drapes his neck across the female's neck. On land the swan pair will engage in a courting dance, gracefully circling each other and flapping their wings.

The pen signals that she is ready to accept the mating act by flattening herself on the water, neck extended. After the male mounts in copulation, they arch necks, half rise, press breast to breast, snort loudly, and then resume their natural positions on the water.

Although mutes usually mate for life, all swans are individuals, and their life-styles sometimes differ. For example, one fickle female showed her independence over a period of six years by annexing three territories and taking four mates. As a general rule, however, 85 percent of swan pairs do not change or abandon mates unless death intervenes; then either male or female may remate. But that doesn't happen immediately; it's often a matter of wait and see, and frequently the new mating doesn't take and the mateless swan remains single.

Swans obviously are birds of character, with loyalty one of their strongest traits. They even work together in building the nest. The female masterminds the work, but again, the male mute is outstanding, being the only male swan that will incubate the eggs while the female bathes, feeds or exercises in a brief flight.

Most birdlife, including even inquisitive and mate-seeking mutes, avoid the territory of a pair of breeding mutes, or even a pair that are beginning to mate, whether they are domestic swans on a pond, or wild. Mutes have the strongest territorial instincts of all swans, never fleeing or avoiding an encounter with an intruder, be it man or beast. In contrast, the big trumpeter will often abandon mate, nest and young if danger threatens. The only other swan that matches the battling mute is the black swan.

Swan expert Sylvia Bruce Wilmore believes that some of the most spectacular battles among birds take place between male mute swans, and she describes such encounters that she has witnessed:

The aggressive swan pounds through the water after an intruder, using simultaneous foot strokes and raising the elbows so that the secondary and tertiary feathers form a graceful arch over the back, and at the same time pressing his neck well down and throwing his head back. Upon meeting the intruder he turns his flank toward him, bows his head and erects his neck feathers, at the same time hissing and moving his head from side to side. The two swans fight breast to breast, often with their necks entwined and beating each other with their powerful wings. These battles can continue until they are exhausted, or one of the birds is injured. The ultimate intention of the aggressor is to push the other's head underwater and attempt to drown him. The aggressive posture is assumed also for intruders of other species—but only within the swan's territory. Once the aggressor is outside his own territory he will draw his feathers close to his body in the submissive posture which he uses in time of fear or when mating.

When the male has driven off the intruder he will return to his mate, and in triumph they meet breast to breast, then stretch their necks, and at times the male will gently rub his neck against his mate's before returning to normal. Their victory is expressed vocally by a prolonged snorting.

The construction of that zealously protected nest begins when the male drops the material—reed stems, rushes, sticks—where the nest will be built. The female arranges the nest gatherings along with what she has collected in a crisscross base, forming the exterior. She then adds to the interior finer vegetation and down that she plucks from her body. Later she will weave in some feathers.

Then, in a motion curiously resembling a sit-down dance, she enters the finished nest, swaying and rocking her body, shuffling her feet, and shaping an eight-inch-deep depression in the center of the nest.

Size varies according to the amount of material gathered, but nests average three to five feet in diameter and one to two feet in height. Swans are very alert to the danger of a nest flooding if it is built near water, and they will construct it extra high to protect their eggs.

Prior to any construction, however, both male and female carefully scout prospective nest sites before making a final selection. They like the quiet waters of lakes and marshes, not disturbed by strong currents or waves. Some instinctively prefer the nearby shallow waters of lakes, ponds, or marshes, where it will not be difficult to dig for water plants and their roots and tubers. Privacy is paramount so abandoned muskrat houses or beaver lodges are favored; however, the water must be of sufficient depth and uncluttered so they can land and take off without problems. Small uninhabited islands are also popular.

Swans also build on land in secluded sites that are surrounded by high grass or reedbeds, or among the protective cover of high bushes or trees. They prefer, however, to build near enough to water so they can easily reach their watery runways for a quick and safe takeoff. They can take off from land if necessary but are more vulnerable there than they are on the water where they are masters.

Mistress of the nest and her brood, the female lays an oval-shaped 12-ounce egg, grayish and tinged with blue-green. She lays one every other day, averaging six, but she can lay as many as a dozen. Laying is usually completed early in April—sooner in the South—and the incubation begins seriously when the last egg is laid. It normally requires about 35 days for the eggs to hatch.

Turning the eggs as they switch nest positions

Remarkably attentive to the incubation, the female rarely leaves the nest, except for very short periods. At this time the male takes her place for incubation duty. Mute males are especially loyal in this regard. There are cases where the mute male, upon the death of his mate, has assumed the entire incubation task and even reared the young. Always, however, during the entire incubation period, while not on nest duty the male is on constant guard duty nearby.

As they switch nest positions, swans turn the eggs to equalize the warmth of incubation. The swan leaving the nest gracefully steps completely clear of it, and when reentering the nest, the swan carefully backs onto it to avoid stepping on the eggs and perhaps crushing them. Care and attention to duty are swan watchwords.

The newborn cygnets rest briefly after hatching, an ordeal of cracking the hard eggshells with the aid of a special needle-sharp egg tooth. When their pale grayish, almost silver, down is dry, the precocial chicks, weighing about seven ounces and born with their eyes open and their bodies covered with protective down, can, as soon as they dry, run, swim and feed themselves.

The mother keeps them in the nest for two days, then the father takes the first-hatched for a swim, alertly watching them and continuing until he has the whole brood swimming, but only for brief periods before they are returned to the nest and the apprehensive mother who checks them out carefully.

The second week is the dangerous period for cygnets. As well as they are protected, one study showed, it is not unusual for 50 percent of the chicks to die before the age of flight. Cold, wet weather kills some, while others may get entangled in water plants and drown. Leeches and internal parasites take their toll, as do big fish like pikes, and turtles, foxes and mink.

Mainly, though, parental care is so excellent that, all factors being equal, the chicks stand a good chance of survival. Solicitude and vigilance are the parental key words. The family swims together and stays together, the female leading, the male keeping a keen eye on the brood from the rear.

For a while the cygnets nibble on the plants the adults bring up from the water, but they are learning now to feed themselves, and within a week of their birth they plunge their heads underwater searching for plant life. In less than two weeks they do the looking-for-food, bottoms-up, heads-beneath-the-water, tip-up technique. Feeding occupies much of the swan's time, especially that of the young. It has been estimated that young swans must increase their weight about 30 times within 100 days to attain the stage of flight.

The cygnets also may get the most rewarding free ride in the bird world. When they are tired, cold or frightened, they have strong, broad backs to lean on. Literally. The adults often encourage their young to climb on their backs, which enables the cygnets to move under their parents' wings for warmth and protection. They even cuddle in the down. Security for young swans is a warm, mobile feather blanket.

The chicks board their parents' backs by hoisting themselves up on the conveniently lowered adult tail, then clutching the feathers to haul themselves into the down hollow of the big backs. When they are in position, the adults curve their wings, forming a protective cradle.

The cygnets communicate with their parents with a series of cheepings: If lost, the young stand as erect as they can and cry loudly. When they are cold and hungry, the cry grows louder, more insistent. When they are tired, the cheeping is soft, quivering. If a chick is hurt, the cry becomes a scream. The mother replies to all of her chicks' cheeps with her own low, soft call and immediately goes to them.

The most dangerous period for the swan family occurs during moulting time when the adults cannot fly. But nature comes to their aid. The breeding female loses her flight feathers about the time her eggs hatch; thus she conveniently and protectively stays on the water with her young for about one month. At about the time she can fly again, the male moults and becomes flightless. This timed moulting means that one parent can fly during the entire brooding period.

It's also a family affair when the young learn to fly; both parents fly with them until they know their way about and gain confidence in their wings and flying ability. Well fed and pampered, the young grow quickly. By the end of five months the gray down vanishes and is replaced with brownish-gray plumage and the important stiff flight feathers which enable the young to fly. It takes over a year, however, for swans to become white (or black). At a year they are still either grayish or brown, depending upon the species. They don't get their adult feathers until they are well into their second year.

Although swans remain in their tight little family groups until after the young can fly well, they are social and do seem to enjoy gathering with larger numbers of birds—but only their own kind. Mutes stay with mutes, whistlers with whistlers, trumpeters with trumpeters; they are a closed society. Thus, although they seem to enjoy sailing along on water alone, or in pairs, they will often join their own groups, even forming impressive flotillas.

Swans on a body of water will belligerently watch a flock of geese or ducks fly over as if daring them to land. And it is seldom that their territory is trespassed. Other birdlife seem aware that swans like to remain secure in their own domain.

Why the constant aggressive vigilance? Swans are protecting not only territory and their own privacy, but their fuzzy, vulnerable young.

They have full responsibility for the welfare of the next generation, enabling it to fly into the proud world of wildlife's most exclusive feathered fraternity.

INDEX